The Twenty-One Semdzins

*With translation of Longchemba's original verses,
seminal instruction from Chogyal Namkhai Norbu
and commentary from Keith Dowman.*

Dzogchen Now! Books

2019

A *Dzogchen Now!* Book
www.keith.dowman@gmail.com

© Keith Dowman 2019

All rights reserved. No part of this book may be reproduced in any form or by any means, electronic or mechanical, including photography, recording, or by any information storage or retrieval system or technologies now known or later developed without permission in writing from the publisher.

ISBN-: 9781709208393

Printed in the U.S.A.
Font set in Baskerville 10.5

Contents

Introduction 6

Part One: Pith Precepts of the Twenty-One Semdzins 15

Part Two: Commentary on the Semdzin Precepts

The First Series: Calming the Mind

    1/1 The Semdzin of the White 'A' 21

    1/2 The Semdzin of the Syllable PHAT. 26

    1/3 The Semdzin of the Heruka's Joyful Laughter 31

    1/4 The Semdzin of the Titan's Struggle. 34

    1/5 The Semdzin of the Long and Short HŪNGs,
    the Thought-Pursuing HŪNGs 38

    1/6 The Semdzin of the Syllable RAM 40

    1/7 The Semdzin of Vajrasattva's Body 42

Second Series: Freedom From Attachment

2/1 The Semdzin of the Pink Pearl Between the Eyes 46

    2/2 The Semdzin of the Three Staffs,
    The Semdzin of the Arrow and Noose 48

    2/3 Semdzin of the White Sphere 51

    2/4 Semdzin of the Rainbow Body 52

    2/5 The Semdzin of Transference 53

    2/6 The Semdzin of Ear Consciousness. 54

2/7 The Semdzin of Vajrasattva in the Heart Centre. 55

The Third Series: Revealing The Nature of Mind

3/1 The Semdzin of the Gradual Revelation of Emptiness 61

3/2 The Semdzin of Immediate Emptiness   65

3/3 The Semdzin of Impermanence   67

3/4 The Semdzin of the Five Great Elements   70

3/5 The Semdzin of Nonthought   72

3/6 The Semdzin of Union   73

3/7 The Semdzin of Space as the Path   77

Appendix 81

Introduction

Nonmeditation is the essential unique Dzogchen meditation. For nonmeditation to kick in, the natural flow of consciousness can be dammed by what we call 'semdzins'. Semdzins 'hold' the mind momentarily, during which time the window to the nature of mind is thrown open or enlarged and nonmeditation proceeds. The most efficient function of the semdzin may lie in the discharge of a misguided effort to inhibit the natural flow of nonmeditation.

Longchemba collected together the twenty-one semdzins in the 14th century and wrote the short descriptions of them in his Dzo Dun. In that all-inclusive tome, the twenty-one were presented as separate but commensurate, categorized, as they are here, under three headings according to three specific and graduated functions. Those three purposes are pacifying the mind, releasing attachment and revealing the nature of mind. This categorization, appearing somewhat intellectually partial and arbitrary, need not be accepted uncritically dogmatically and practised accordingly. Indeed, once the twenty-one semdzins have become familiar according to Longchemba's rubric they can be utilized at will, all equal as gateways into the nature of mind and the basis of experimental meditation.

Nonmeditation is the sole crucial method of Dzogchen meditation, yet nonmeditation cannot be programmed or devised. These twenty-one semdzins are all the same or similar open-sesame keys to that nonmeditation, meditations that *allow* or *enable* nonmeditation, or 'make space for' nonmeditation.' The natural flow of consciousness is dammed by the semdzin and mind is 'held' momentarily, during which time the window to the nature of mind is thrown open, or enlarged, and nonmeditation proceeds with clarity. A powerful head of energy may be built up behind the dam of discipline, and particular mindforms may be engendered, such as high awareness with varying degrees of bliss, radiance, thoughtlessness and/or emptiness. But these experiences are secondary and irrelevant to the central concern, which is nonmeditation. In this way the semdzins remove obstacles to naturally-arising nonmeditation rather than create the conditions for it.

Many of the exercises herein may be found on mahayana and some even on hinayana paths, but in these lesser, causal, vehicles, a relative, temporal, goal is anticipated and when the anticipated end is achieved it is greeted with a sense of success and attainment—another, higher, rung on the ladder has been reached. On the contrary, in Dzogchen, in the case of every semdzin, the already extant, undeniable, nondual refuge is the outcome.

It is vital that these semdzins are not conceived as 'method'. Indeed, the possibility of any Dzogchen realization—nonmeditation—is thwarted by any apperceptive idea of attainment. Likewise, the idea that nonattainment is the 'method' of attainment of realization can trip us up. It must not be given any positivistic status that can turn it into an objective aim. Neither nonmeditation nor nonattainment can be objectified by 'the knower', or the intellect, without undermining its actuality— its authenticity. That is the nature of the nondual. If the semdzins takes us to a place where we no longer hanker after attainment or nonattainment and thus allow Dzogchen to seep into our no-longer-desirous intellects then their function is realized. So, put aside the idea that these exercises provide a ladder to

Dzogchen attainment. If they alleviate the pressures of samsara to the extent that we give up all thought of spiritual accomplishment, then they have been particularly useful. If they provide a non-temporal gap through which the natural light of the mind may shine, they will have proved thrir worth.

If the dangerous elevation of the positivistic effects of the semdzins to concepts of 'meditation' and 'practise'—always imminent —becomes acute, then it is probably best to ignore their practice and move on immediately to Dzogchen nonmeditation or the Dzogchen preliminaries. The dangers inherent in making practise of the semdzins a habit may well provide the reason why Longchemba spent so little time in their exegesis. If this warning is taken to heart and the semdzins are rejected as 'method', if they are spurned as steps up to a diving board, as it were, from where we can launch ourselves into the nature of mind, take also the warning that it is as equally dangerous to use them as support along the way when we find ourselves in an apparently inescapable dualistic dug-out. The answer to both situations is the complete relaxation that is nonaction, 'or doing nothing', rather than a return to the already rejected positivistic methodology of vajrayana.

So although these semdzin are not to be practiced as part of a fixed regular sadhana, it may be advisable to undertake a short retreat or a period of intense engagement with each of them, several of them, or one of them, to gain lucidity and familiarity. Dedicated practice will provide the familiarization needed to enter into any of them effortlessly when required and the ability to let go of them immediately—or at least at the end of the period of practice. Their perfect utility is accomplished when one or another of the twenty-one comes into mind spontaneously during nonmeditation and is immediately and effectively activated. Then they will be included in regular sitting sessions.

In the initial period of assimilation, practice whatever of the twenty-one semdzins is intuited as part of the flow, one alone, or two or more in succession, in any order, or the whole twenty-one from beginning to end. Giving more or less time, an hour or a week or a month to each, one after the other, until they arise fluently whenever they are required.

When the semdzins have been assimilated, each yogin/yogini will have his or her own personal preferences amongst the semdzins, more experience having been gained with some than with others, some always seemingly applicable and making perfect sense, arising spontaneously and clearly and usefully. Others will arise only occasionally or not at all. Sometimes, in a kind of lacunae, these semdzins are like water off a duck's back—we just do not get it. So be sure that nonmeditation—simply sitting—is the main point and the semdzins only our back-up.

Perhaps the intervention of a lama prescribing what is most relevant for one's own mind is a more economical and expedient manner of proceeding, and such a lama may be able to provide personalized instruction. If a lama who knows you well is not available, then take Longchenpa's instruction to heart and fill it out with Chogyal Namkhai Norbu's comments. The Commentary consists both of definitive and provisional instruction, 'definitive' insofar as it elaborates the sometimes scant Tibetan rubric, and 'provisional' in that it posits varied approaches—different strokes for different folks— to the same end.

The first part of this publication provides a translation of Longchen Rabjampa's essential instruction on the twenty-one semdzins. The second, commentarial, part provides the Tibetan original in transliteration, a translation of it, relevant comments from the late Chogyal Namkhai Norbu, and an oral commentary given by Keith Dowman at a seminar at Staufen in Germany in 2011. That oral commentary has been thoroughly edited but the colloquial element is still quite plain. The several references to the 'rushen' in the text refer to the Dzogchen preliminaries described in Jigmelingpa's *Yeshe Lama* and translated under that title and published as a Dzogchen Now! Book.

Again, finally, it is imperative that the semdzins are not perceived as a means to a temporal end. In such a case they are reduced to rungs on an endless ladder stretching up to heaven, and Dzogchen becomes merely a name for another school of Mahayana Buddhism. Insofar as we perceive Dzogchen as a means to an end rather than the end itself, and insofar as we see that end as separate from the nature of our actual state of mind in the here and now, we demean it, reducing it to another religious enterprise. Dzogchen is not an escape from the maelstrom of everyday life; it is the total acceptance of whatever comes down, whatever it may be, so that total unitary identity is assured—no particle remaining separate and unassimilated—and simultaneously at one with the nature of that experience, which is the nature of mind.

Pith Precepts of the Twenty-One Semdzins

1. To Attain a Peaceful Balanced Mindset

1/1 The Semdzin of the White 'A'
Visualize a white, luminous, 'A' on the tip of the nose. On the outbreath the 'A' moves away; on the inbreath the 'A' returns mixed with the breath. Training day and night in this manner the extraordinary experience of freedom from mental quiescence and activity (mental emanation and absorption) arises.

1/2 The Semdzin of the Syllable PHAT
If you get tired exclaim the syllable PHAT: sometimes let consciousness run free and then forcefully enunciate that syllable. A state of consciousness of thoughtless amazement will arise and the mind is held as pure presence (*rikpa*) until another thought arises at which time again enunciate the syllable PHAT. Practising this through night and day the meditation of empty luminous mind in its natural condition arises.

1/3 The Semdzin of the Heruka's Joyful Laughter
Joyfully laugh the exclamation HA, short and forcefully (start with one and increase to five), and as with the exclamation PHAT the mind is secured and the experience of thoughtfree clarity arises.

1/4 The Semdzin of the Titan's Struggle
Sit in an exposed place and in seclusion, and holding your knees to the chest first turn your head one way and then the other, and then turn your shoulders and shoulders and torso.

Together. Keep your knees to your chest as tightly as possible and turn strenuously, forcefully. Outer appearances will be shot through with successive colours until appearances cease by themselves and whatever arises—which is to say your vision—will be indefinable, and the experience of self-liberating appearances arises.

1/5 The Semdzin of the Long and Short HŪNGs or the
    Thought-Pursuing HŪNGs
Identify long resonant vocalized HŪNGs with the breath and when intractable thoughts or thought-trains arise use the short exclamation HŪNG to disperse them. Unmoving from our original condition experience of clarity of the nature of thought arises.

1/6 The Semdzin of the Syllable RAM
Visualize the syllable RAM in the navel centre, bright, radiant, translucent, red in colour, glowing and then burning. Fixate on the syllable. Sound the syllable softly as you visualize it. Heat arises.

1/7 The Semdzin of the Deity's Body
Visualize oneself as Vajrasattva; visualize Vajrasattva on the tip of the nose, mix that visualization with the outbreath and inbreath; visualize an infinite number of Vajrasattvas emanating from the pores of the skin and the nine bodily orifices on the inbreath and returning on the outbreath. With an attentive mind the experience of consciousness as magnificent pure luminosity arises.

2. To Attain Detachment

2/1 The Semdzin of the Pink Pearl
Focus the mind on a white/red sphere the size of a pea between the eye brows. Experiences of energy will arise thereby.

2/2 The Semdzin of the Three Staffs: The Arrow and Noose
The central channel, and the *roma* (left) and *kyangma??* (right) are like straight staffs down the centre of the body, the right and left channels exiting at the nostrils: exhale forcefully like

shooting an arrow, expelling all disease, faults and errors with it, and then inhaling catch the prana as with a lasso and insert it into the central channel at the junction four fingers below the navel. Rising up the central channel through the four chakras, the *prana* suffuses the body with awareness. Experiences of the empty clarity of pure presence (*rikpa*) arise.

2/3 The Semdzin of the White Sphere
On the tip of the nose is a prana sphere that is carried away for a metre to a kilometre by the exhalation and brought back by the inhalation. Focus on this and you will experience thoughtless clarity.

2/4 The Semdzin of the Rainbow Body
Visualize a small white 'A' in the heart centre and focus unwaveringly on a net of five-colour rainbow light — translucent, clear, insubstantial emanating from it in all directions bounded by the sphere in which you sit. You experience the pure clear light.

2/5 The Semdzin of Transference
Visualize a ball of light on the fontanelle filled up with all mind and energy that with the sound of the syllable HŪNG rises into space moving higher and higher in the sky until it vanishes altogether. In this way you experience emptiness beyond thought.

2/6 The Semdzin of Ear Consciousness
Focus attention in the ear and relax. Thereby you will experience the samadhi of sound.

2/7 The Semdzin of Kuntuzangpo in the Heart
Focus upon the tiny form of Kuntuzangpo (Samantabhadra) in a globe of blue light in the heart centre. Thereby you will experience pure clear light, and you will cultivate the clear light of the bardo, and at death there will be buddha deity, relics (ringsel) and rainbow light.

3. To Reveal the Nature of Mind

3/1 The Semdzin of The Gradual Revelation of Emptiness
Through discursive and experiential analysis of appearances and ego, arrive at the emptiness of both objective and subjective aspects of experience. Finally, without any mentation, the experience of nondual emptiness arises.

3/2 The Semdzin of Immediate Emptiness
Gaze intently at whatever appears and regard it as utterly pure and empty. Applying this to all forms and all sounds, etc, all appearances are experienced like condensation on a mirror.

3/3 The Semdzin of Impermanence
Regard appearances without any centrality of focus, without solid ground, without any invariable point of reference, uncertain, undependable, always variable. Whatever arises, appearing in a variable and non-veridical variety, is thus seen as delusion (a lie) and utterly indeterminate. Training in impermanence brings experience of freedom from grasping.

3/4 The Semdzin of the Five Great Elements
Focus consciousness unwaveringly without any distraction upon whatever of the five elements appears as earth and rock, ice, water or steam, fire, air or wind, or space. You experience self-liberation in that place of focus like dream experience.

3/5 The Semdzin of Thoughtlessness
Whatever appearance arises in consciousness, whatever moves in the necklace-sequence of instants, intuitively apprehend the indivisible, thoughtfree ultimate place. Holding the mind in this way the samadhi of intrinsic nonthought arises.

3/6 The Semdzin of Union
At the arising of dualistic appearances (subject/object, inside/outside) gaze intently at the crux (totality) of that polarity and the experience of the serene intrinsic purity of

nonduality will arise. Also, by taking the bliss of male and female buddha-union as the path the experience of nondual bliss and emptiness arises.

3/7 The Semdzin of Space as the Path
Visualize pure presence (*rikpa*) as vanished into space, and visualise all appearances and mind as floating in the space unsupported, and visualize the space as all things.
Experience of great boundless emptiness arises.

Commentary on the Semdzin Precepts

The First Series: Calming the Mind

Bdun tsan dang pos rang sems gnas du gzhung pa.

The seven parts of the first series bring the mind back home; the mind settles into quiescence.

NB: The mind comes home, resumes its natural place (*rang sems gnas du gzhung ba*).

CNN: We attain the calm state of shinay (*zhi gnas*).

Commentary
Shinay is but a preliminary state in which emptiness, nonthought, and clarity can develop. Shinay is not Dzogchen or an end in itself: the semdzin of the various methods of holding the mind provide an occasion for understanding the nature of mind, i.e. *rikpa*. The stated goals of all three series are implicit in each.

1 / 1 The Semdzin of the White 'A'

Dang po la bdun gyi gzung ba ni: A dkar la sems gzung ba ni: gnas yid dang mthun par stan bde la lus skyil krung gis 'dug ste sna rtser a dkar la 'tser ba cig bsgoms nas rlung phir gro dus a yang phar song nang du 'gengs dus a yang tshur byung bar bsams la rlung dang bsres te bsgoms mo. De yang lus la tshad nad yod na 'A' de grang reg grang nad la tsha reg tu bsams la nyin mtshan du sbyangs bas sems spro bsdu dang bral ba'i nyams myong thun mong ma yin pa skye'o. Lus gnad rlung gnad thams cad la 'dra'o.

The first of the seven is the semdzin of the white 'A': In a pleasant place, on a comfortable seat, sitting in lotus posture, visualize a white luminous 'A' on the tip of the nose. On the out-breath, the 'A' moves away; on the in-breath, the 'A' returns mixed with the breath. When the body feels unpleasantly hot, visualize the 'A' as cool; when the body feels too cool, visualize it as hot. Training day and night in this manner the extraordinary experience of freedom from mental quiescence and activity (mental projection and absorption) arises.

The important points of body and breathing are to be sustained in all the subsequent exercises.

NB. Visualize the Tibetan 'A' or Roman A? Of the Three Tibetan A-s: the first is simply the opening of the glottis: freedom from mental quiescence and activity, from mental emanation and absorption (*sems spro bsdu, gnas rgyu rig gsum*).

CNN: We do it until we don't have to think about the visualization and movement.

Commentary

The first semdzin of the entire series is the semdzin of the white 'A'. The practice is simple. On the tip of the nose visualize the letter 'A'. The letter is radiant white in colour. On each out-breath send the visualized letter out to about a metre. On each in-breath bring it back to the tip of the nose. That is all. The letter 'A' is not articulated.

The distance of projection of the letter 'A' can be extended up to two or three metres. In this we may find that when the 'A' reaches its maximum extension at the end of the out-breath we will pause momentarily, and likewise when it comes back and touches the nose at the end of the in-breath again there will be a pause.

The size of the 'A'? If it is too big, then on its return it might miss the nose altogether and hit your face. On the other hand, if it is too small, we might breathe it in. So, the answer is not too big and not too small.

We may wonder whether the breath should be passed through the nose or the mouth. There is no focus on one or the other, but there is a natural use of both channels, because the nasal aspect of it takes the air through the nose, whereas the aspiration sends it through the mouth. So, we start through the nose, then end up through the mouth. But it can be both, more or less, all the time.

Let's not confuse this 'A' with the ĀH in OM ĀH HŪNG. It comes from a different place in the throat. There are three A-s to recognize in the Tibetan alphabet. The first, 'A', is made by opening the glottis and passing air through the vocal cords before any sound is articulated. Putting the air into first gear produces the short vowel *a* which is the sound of the *a* in the Roman alphabet. The third is the long ĀH in OM ĀH HŪNG. It is the first one that we are concerned with here.

Consider the symbolic importance of the 'A': Insofar as we cannot sound, speak or utter anything without opening the glottis, this 'A' is the root of all sounds. Insofar as there is no real sound in that letter, it does not represent a sound, but only a potential sound It is called the 'unborn sound' and symbolizes potential reality. The nature of Dzogchen reality is always and only unborn. It can never come into full existence and in this sense, reality cannot exist. But then on the other hand it neither exists nor does it not exist. And since it neither exists, nor not exist, it does not come into being. And if it does not come into being, then it cannot cease to be. In this way the reality that 'A' represents is considered always to be only potential. This avoids making any conventional logical statement about the nature of its existence, which is beyond rational thought, beyond the intellect, beyond conception. This exercise may appear to be very simple, but it is loaded.

The Tibetan letter 'A' is not easy to visualize, so for beginners perhaps the roman letter A is to be preferred. But we are none of us beginners here, so I strongly recommend that we visualize this Tibetan glyph. Every calligraphic Tibetan 'A' is different; we won't find two the same, so our visualization of it can never be wrong. But there is a movement of the brush or the knife, when writing or cutting these letters, that makes heavy on the top and lighter and thinner below. The script is called (*dbu-chen*), meaning 'heavy head', which is why one can say that the weight lies at the top.

We will find our own 'A', and at the beginning, as long as we see the rough shape in the visualization, that is sufficient.

The instruction is to mix the visualization with the breath, to mix 'the mind with the breath'. The shape of the syllable is mind-created, and it comes mixed with the in-breath and the out-breath. Gross breath, subtle energy and mind all function together in this semdzin of visualization of the white 'A'. The mind created white 'A' is mixed with the gross breath and subtle energy. The connection between breathing, mind and subtle energy is of vital importance.

Concentration is primary in this semdzin. Concentration—'fixation on an object'—is the basic method of bringing the mind back into its natural place, which is a calm place. This is *shinay* in Tibetan, which literally means 'peaceful place' (*shamatā* in Sanskrit). The focal function in the exercise is dominant. But at the same time, we are watching a moving object. There is a dynamic sensory element to the meditation. The breath and the energy are tied to the object.

Firstly, concentrate on the visualization, and according to your capacity to visualize, concentrated focus will go into that process of visualization. Secondly, concentrated energy goes into mixing the breath with the mind-created syllable. Thirdly, concentrated energy goes into the degree of extension of the breath with the syllable and sound that it carries and also into its return. In this way we reinforce the natural propensity of the mind to concentrate, and the result is a very peaceful, absorbed, state.

This exercise is an application of shinay. Shinay leads to concentrated absorption. The state of concentrated absorption is called *samadhi*; there are four stages of this process of samadhi according to the tradition. The four stages of absorption are first grasping the object of focus, the second is fixation on the object of focus, the third is going into or beyond the object and attaining bliss, and the fourth going into the state of perfect equanimity, the peaceful state, which is called the samadhi of shamatā.

This exercise reinforces the mind's tendency to concentrate. This is not Dzogchen. It is a very useful state to be able to achieve, because hereby we can reach equilibrium, re-adjusting imbalance.

Longchemba recommends that this exercise is practised in an intensive retreat situation. 'By working at this practice night and day, the extraordinary experience which is free from projection and absorption arises.' Projection—all forms of mental activity that are extroversive—and absorption, an introversive function, are transcended in this ideal concentration. Projection leads to complete dispersion; absorption ultimately leads to stasis. So 'beyond projection and absorption' means transcending the processes of the mind.

Concentration is only the first benefit of this semdzin. The higher and longer-term result, according to Longchemba, is the meditative freedom from the dichotomy of projection and absorption, from the concentration and mindfulness of shinay and lhaktong.

1/2 The Semdzin of the Syllable PHAT

De la skyo na yi ge PHAT *sems gzung ba ni: dar cig shes pa yeng du bcug la* PHAT *ches drag po brjod pas shes pa rtog med had de be chig 'ong ba la rtog pa ma langs kyi bar sems bzung la yang* PHAT *ches nying mthan du nyams su blangs bas sems stong gsal rang gdangs kyi sgom pa skye'o*

If and when you are tired, sound the PHAT: sometimes [let consciousness run free] and then forcefully enunciate the syllable PHAT. A state of consciousness of thoughtless amazement (*hadewa*) arises and until another thought follows, the mind is held [in a state of *rikpa*]; into each successive thought enunciate the syllable PHAT. Experiencing this through night and day the meditation of empty luminous mind in its natural condition arises.

NB: Thoughtless amazement is *hadewa:* empty, disoriented, disassociated. This is to be allowed—do not try and remain unaffected. PHAT: PHA signifies method (*thabs*); TA signifies wisdom (*shes rab*): the sanctity of PHAT.

CNN: The effect can be increased by fixating first on an object or point in space, which is like holding the breath, and after a few seconds relaxing and allowing thought to arise, and then uttering PHAT. *Perform the exercise a few times in succession. Here* rikpa *and the calm state are one.*

Commentary
The second semdzin is the semdzin of the syllable PHAT. Mark that the first semdzin is the semdzin of the white 'A'.

This PHAT which is of immense importance in Dzogchen practice is only the second. This indicates the importance of the 'A' rather than the secondary status of the PHAT. Why is the 'A' more important? Longchemba does not comment on this, but surely not only do we have no concentration meditation, but we have no meditation at all unless we have some inborn degree of concentration. We cannot meditate with a dispersed mind, or extroversive mind, unless we have some concentration; the distinction made here is between being totally spaced-out and being spaced-out with attention. Lhaktong (*vipassana*), for instance, is an extroversive meditation; the meditation of putting our consciousness successively at the five doors of the senses and watching is an 'insight' exercise. But we cannot do it without concentration.

It was Sakyamuni's genius that connected awareness with breathing. Maybe somebody will take objection to that—the *pranayama* of Patanjali is also very powerful meditation exercises. But Patanjali didn't talk about attention or awareness.

We have experienced the syllable PHAT through the lama's utterance when he gave the pointing out instruction. There are two ways to experience it, hearing the sound from outside, or listening to our own utterance. First of all, as Patrul Rinpoche's makes clear in his *Tsiksum Nedek* instruction, the syllable PHAT is an initiatory device. At the same time, it is a method of breaking thought-trains. These two functions are intimately linked. We discover the importance and function of the syllable PHAT through our own experience.

The way to sound the PHAT is explosive. It is difficult to make it anything but explosive; the nature of the word is like an explosive ejaculation. But we enunciate it in such a way that it creates the optimal amount of shock in the mind. The enunciation of the syllable PHAT creates a split second of shock, which is startled consciousness. The Tibetan word *hadewa* denotes just that moment of amazement, or startled wonder. Following the moment of shock, is a moment of thoughtlessness. In the moment of shock perhaps we 'lose consciousness' as awareness is shattered, but in the following moment awareness arises again in thoughtlessness, but there is in that thoughtlessness a consciousness: we have awareness. We have awareness, we have *rikpa*, we have presence. In that moment, we have intimation of 'awareness of the nature of mind'.

The first moment in the wake of the sound PHAT is 'empty mind'. In that empty mind *rikpa* can arise. The syllable PHAT is like the gate to *rikpa*. The notion here of the 'first moment' is vital; liberation is intrinsic to the first moment. In that first moment *rikpa* can spontaneously arise. Thus, we use involuntary—out-of-control—thought processes as the means to awareness. A train of non-talkers spins out of control and the attachment provides the opportunity for identification with the nature of mind.

Enunciation of the syllable PHAT solves 'the problem' of thought, which may be stated as 'the thought of the solution prevents its arising'. What is undeniable about thought is that it always implies mental activity. Thought can probably be heralded as the mark of being human. We can have gaps between thoughts, and we can have an empty centre of thought, but thought still remains. What is notable about thought is that like reality itself, attachment to it is very painful. In other words, if we believe our thoughts to be real and true, we have serious problems. The sound of the PHAT releases us from thought-attachment.

Of course, we may rationalize that we cannot trust thought. First of all because it is inconsistent, because it expresses itself in terms of opposing concepts, because it presents contrary arguments regarding the same problems at different times. We cannot trust thought because it is a function of emotion; it is basically unbelievable; it is naturally judgemental; it constantly produces conflicting opinions. Objective attention to our thought patterns should convince us that they are generally untrustworthy. It is the attachment to the conclusions that rest upon our thinking, however, and that is the problem, that is where the pain lies. There is no reliable and constant way to stop it, however, without the PHAT. And, thereafter, as it should have become clear, in Dzogchen there is no will to change, no alteration, no destruction, no cutting away—and no cultivation.

The PHAT is used as an initiatory symbol in the pointing out instruction when the lama introduces the nature of mind. When we use the syllable ourselves, we are giving auto-initiation. At least, in that split second, we can gain an intimation of the nature of mind, in that post-shock awareness, and that intimation has vital importance. It is initiatory; we gain a touchstone. It is this touchstone that is reinforced constantly in every subsequent intimation. As intimation follows intimation, confidence is engendered in the nature of Dzogchen experience as pure potential, in there being nothing else in truth except that reality. As confidence becomes conviction, there is reinforcement, which is a growing sense of Dzogchen experience. Just in case we come to believe that Dzogchen experience is anything unusual, then remember that in a manner of speaking it is 'ordinary sensory experience'. This suggests the analogy of climbing the mountain only to return to the starting point, to base camp, so that we may be able to recognize its reality for the first time.

If somebody else does it for us, we can call it an initiatory ritual. If we do it ourselves then it is a practical technique that is eminently portable and that we can use at any time. This second semdzin can be employed anytime in the waking state.

Further, the meaning of the word semdzin becomes clearer here: the visualization of the white 'A' and the exclamation of PHAT are two completely different experiences but they have in common the function of 'holding the mind'.

Now, look at the traditional analysis of the syllable PHAT. It is a two-in-oneness paradigm. Two in oneness (*zung-'jug*) is a tantric notion, but it is also used in Dzogchen. The syllable 'PHAT' is made up of two phonemes. The first, PHA, represents skilful means; and the second, TA, represents insight into the nature of all things as emptiness. To provide a metaphysical analysis of that, 'the PHA is the form, the method, and the unsounded TA represents the nature of form as wisdom. It is known also as 'the sunderer' or 'the cutter', and that may relate to the word 'trekcho' which means 'cutting through'.

But look for the initiatory effect in the wake of any startling sound—the slamming of a door, the smash of china on the kitchen floor, an aeroplane passing through the sound barrier, or a sudden breaking of wind.

Then consider the sanctity of these syllables: all these syllables—PHAT, HUNG and 'A'—will work for us only insofar as we retain the sense of their sanctity. Treat them with disrespect, sit on them, or use them in a profane context, and they lose their potency. Of course, they have no intrinsic worth over any other sounds, or any other sacred symbol whatsoever. But these working symbols have been endowed with special significance by the tradition over a millennium; they are tools that we can work with, and a workman respects his tools.

As a rule, the PHAT is disclosed in a ritual form, in a formal initiation, but at any time, whenever we use the word or whenever we hear it, PHAT can have an initiatory effect. For this reason, it should always be treated with immense sanctity. Do not use it out of context, out of meditation, do not discuss it, do not do anything to diminish its power—keep it a secret.

We know, finally, that the sound is used to conclude various exercises. In the practice of the white 'A' for instance, the PHAT is used to finalize it. It puts us back into the relaxed state of mind-watching. Wherever we hear it, we look at the nature of mind and tune into the potential for identifying, recognizing it completely. We can utilize it in any of these semdzin exercises, or in the ngondro, in the Blue HŪNG exercise, for example, or at the end of looking at the source, place and dissolution of thoughts. But in the dedicated semdzin of the syllable PHAT, we are watching the nature of mind; and thoughts are arising, and when the intensity of them or the attachment to them reaches a threshold, at that point we sound the syllable PHAT.

1/3 The Semdzin of the Heruka's Joyful Laughter

Yang khro bo dgyes pa'i gad mo la sems gzung ba ni: HA drag la thung bar brjod la snga ma ltar sems gtad pas rtog med gsal gdams kyi nyams skye'o

The semdzin of wrathful and joyous laughter: Laugh the sound HA short and forcefully and as above (in 1/2) the mind is secured and the experience of thoughtfree clarity arises.

CNN: HA *is the third aspirate in the Tibetan alphabet.* 'A' *is peaceful, HA is wrathful. Start with one* HA, *then two, then up to five.*

Commentary

This is the semdzin of laughter called the joyful laughter of the Heruka. The Heruka is wrathful buddha-deity. The laughter we practise in this semdzin is the joyful laughter of the wrathful deity. Remember that there is no anger or lust in the nature of the wrathful deities. Their nature is 'detached desirous' red in colour, or 'cool aversion' blue in colour, and there is always a lightness about their being. Their essence is emptiness; their nature radiance. Hence the wrathful and yet joyful laughter expressed ritually as HA.

It may be enough to enunciate the syllable once. It can be articulated, however, two, three, or up to seven times. But start with one. It should be sounded short and forceful, but not heavily.

The semdzin should be practised by identifying with Heruka. We cannot use the exclamation to evoke the Heruka. We must *be* the Heruka in order to use the exclamation. Or perhaps, alternatively, the identification with the Heruka and the exclamation are simultaneous? This semdzin is not something to be used very often. Perhaps of all the semdzins it is the one least used—although it may be the most powerful.

Remember that the Heruka's laughter is joyful, but obviously it relates to passion, because passion is the mask of the Heruka. So, it is the sound of recognition of an emotional thought-filled mind.

The syllable HA, the syllable of laughter, is used to cut the thinking/emotional syndrome, in the same way, at the same place, that the PHAT is used. It is used the same way as the PHAT, an emphatic sound short, sharp and compelling that stops thought. Insofar as this semdzin requires more spontaneity than the PHAT, it is more difficult to practise. It is used for the same purpose as PHAT. It is a cutting syllable.

Perhaps it is correct to say that it cuts emotion more than it cuts thought.

The subtleties of the expression that arise spontaneously are not a matter for discussion. Spontaneity cannot be taught and nor can it be improvised.

The Heruka, the wrathful buddha-deity, is central to the entire practice. It is his laughter, and it can only be such laughter if there is recognition of the nature of the Heruka's state of mind. It requires a recognition of the absurdity of human emotion. Without that understanding there is no cause for laughter, and we cannot use the syllable. To employ the semdzin of joyful laughter there is also an assumption that we can sit (or move) in meditation and even momentarily hold that sentiment.

The topic of shouts is dealt with extensively in the mother-tantra, specifically the *Hevajra-tantra*. Here Heruka is Demchok (Chakrasambara) and the syllable is described in terms of seven tones. Longchemba does not mention tones. It is as if the appropriate tone will arise spontaneously in each circumstance, so there is no need to practise it.

There is a mahasiddha story in which the syllable is employed: The yogi Virupa is wandering in the far east of India where the mother-goddess cult was—and still is—particularly strong. He was captured by witches while he slept in the outskirts of a village. These were flesh-eating witches, cannibal witches, and in the morning they were to sacrifice and consume Virupa. But during the night Virupa uses his laughter to paralyze the witches and free himself. The story indicates the power of the sound and its effect in particular circumstances.

Again, this should be treated with respect and used ony in rare circumstances.

1/4 The Semdzin of the Titan's Struggle.

Lha ma yin rtsod pa 'gyed pa la sems gzung ba ni: Ri rtse'am brag steng la sogs par 'dug la lus sgul bskyod dal bar bya. De ltar nyi ma gsum bzhir byas nas drag tu khams kyis thub thang du sgri zhing sgul bskyod byas pas phyi'i snang ba dmar khral khrug dang ser lhang lheng dang sngo gya gyur 'gyur ba dang thim thim 'du 'gyur ba dag skya sang seng 'gyur ba'o. Rjes la phyi'i snang ba rang 'gags nas chi'i ngo bor yang grub pa med par mthong ste mthong snang rang grol ba'i nyams su myong ba skye'o. 'Di'i dus na rlung la shis pa'i kha zas bsten no. Lte bar yi ge ram la sems gtad do.

The Semdzin of the Titan's Struggle: Sitting on a mountain top or on top of a rock, move the body easily [in the posture with knees clasped to chest, turning first the neck with the body following, first to one side and then the other]. Do that for three or four days and then [do the movement more forcefully according to your condition]. Outer appearances will first be shot through with red colour, then yellow, then green becoming spacious and then [blue] beginning to vanish and finally grey becoming invisible. After that outer appearances cease by themselves and we will see the nature of whatever arises, which is to say your vision will be indefinable, and the experience of self-liberating appearance arises. Take food that supports the air humour. Visualize RAM in the navel centre

NB: The titan is an anti-god, a demon (*lha ma yin, asura*).

CNN: Rotate the head from side to side for 15 minutes, strenuously, slow down if you become dizzy; watching appearances, colour sequences arise leaving you in thoughtlessness—emptiness.

Visualize a red RAM *for heat; visualize* RAM *in the knees.*

Commentary

The third semdzin is called the Titan's struggle. This is best done sitting in an exposed place and in seclusion. Sit on the ground and hold your knees to your chest, and first turn your head one way and then the other, and then turn your shoulders, and then shoulders and torso. Keep your knees to your chest held as tightly as possible. When moving the shoulders widely, you must slacken the hold on your knees and let them slip as you turn. Turn as far as possible. Strenuously…forcefully. Remember this exercise is called the struggle of the titan. No benefit will accrue unless you put energy into it. It is a demanding physical struggle, not a symbolic one. Let the eyes lead the movement. First, the eyes and then the head, and then the shoulders.

Remember the title of this semdzin. It is not simply a yoga posture—it is a struggle. Hold on tightly to your knees as firmly as you can; pull them closely to your chest; then starting with your head, move as far to the right as you can, then to the left. That does not entail much struggle, but the more you get into it, the more you move your shoulders, and then you are struggling against yourself. You will find that a rhythm arises. There is no form of breathing specified, but you will fall naturally into a regular pattern of breathing.

No effect is produced unless the struggle is made strenuously, and strenuously means vigorously, particularly in the development with the shoulders. Turn as far as you can, putting muscular power behind both the holding and the turning, and also for as long as you can, for fifteen minutes at least. But do not do yourself damage. Work with it. There are no specific instructions in the literary source, and the oral instruction says, 'work with it'.

We can get different kinds of effects from this. The principal positive effect concerns stimulation of the *nadis* of the subtle-body in the neck—that is how the effect is described. But clearly, relaxation of the body, limbering the body and getting out of the stiff paralysis of meditative posture, loosening up the whole psycho-organism is the result. The effect that is described in the canon is the increase of the sense of illusion.

If the exercise is producing the standard effect, then first the visual field—the environment—will turn red and from red to yellow, yellow to green, green to blue and blue to grey. This is in the visual field, relating to objects of the eye; this is not hallucination or internal experience. The changes in the visionary field will occur at the climax of the yoga as the product of exertion, before relaxation. The struggle of the titan creates a sense of illusion. This illusionary quality arises through a succession of colour: red, yellow, green, blue and grey. Longchemba says the visual field is 'shot through' with colour, so it is not like the entire landscape is to be seen as through red spectacles; rather it is like splashes of colour, lines of colour, like a mist on a TV screen.

The exercise is concluded by letting go and falling supine on the ground. This implies total relaxation, releasing every nerve in the body. This is of crucial importance. The relaxation at the end of every session is the profit of the yoga; in that state we can see the nature of mind.

If dizziness occurs, or any negative physical effect, then stop. Do not push when there is a sign of dysfunction. Fifteen minutes is enough time to spend on it until you have some experience in it. So, for instance, do five minutes with the head, and five minutes head and shoulders together. But do not take these fifteen minutes as an absolute; do it as you feel competent; different bodies are going to react in different ways, more or less, male or female.

This semdzin is a support for various yogas. Perhaps, primarily, it is a support developing the sense of illusion (*maya*), where illusion means a sense of insubstantiality. It also can lead to the experience of thoughtlessness and clarity. The optimal moment for it is after a long period of sitting meditation, when your neck has become stiff and your whole body is feeling rigid, and you need blood coursing through your system again, or you feel need to turn up the oxygen supply.

Consider these three semdzins: The White 'A', the PHAT and the Titan's Struggle. These three yogas do not oppose any process or energy in the body, on the contrary they are reinforcing natural propensities: the natural propensity to concentrate, the natural propensity to cut and move on, and here it is the natural propensity to stretch and relax. The exercise requires an intensive period of practice before we can utilize it optimally within the context of Dzogchen retreat. When we are sitting doing Dzogchen no-mind, the impulse to practise any of these semdzins may arise spontaneously, and that's when we can get the maximum benefit. We cannot get the expected result before the semdzin kicks-in automatically.

We can become quite obsessive and intensive in this practice. The texts suggest that it may be sustained for days on end. Take your seat on a large rock or a hill top, and maintain the practice for a few days—at least, if not the full twenty-four hours, the daylight hours.

The distinction between forcing the yoga and maximizing its potential is very fine. The asura naturally pushes his ambition into the danger zone and likewise we need to go beyond the point of exhaustion in this practice. Taking it to the point where falling totally exhausted—and fully relaxed—into the nature of mind at the end of every session should be the norm.

A warning about diet during the period of this practice: eat well, eat substantial food that provides heat, so that you can keep warm.

1/5 The Semdzin of the Long and Short HŪNGs, the Thought-Pursuing HŪNGs

Rnam rtog HŪNG gis ded pa la sems gzung ba ni: HŪNG *ring ba dbyangs dang bcas pa rlung dang 'dres la sems de'i ngang las gzhan du ma yengs bar bzung la skabs su* HŪNG *thung ba re brjod pas rnam rtog chos nyid du sangs pa'i nyams skye'o*

The semdzin of thought-pursuing HŪNGs: Mixing the long resonant HŪNG with the breath, remain unwavering from the original condition of the mind. When thought arises sometimes sound a short HŪNG and experience of clarity of the nature of thought arises.

CNN: This semdzin is like that of the White 'A'—but stronger. The HŪNG *is as in the* OM ĀH HŪNG *of the Rushen, combining long* HŪNG *(*HŪNG *ring) and short* HŪNG *(*HŪNG *thung) as in Rushen but without visualization. Breathe out through the mouth and the nose. Concentrate on the sound: the calm state arises. Concentrate (fixate) when thoughts arise. When distracted sound* HŪNG *forcefully and loudly several times, then slow down again. When relaxed, sound the short* HŪNG *several times, say five times. Watch the process of thoughts with long and short* HŪNG*s. Try to stop thinking and watch thought multiply: try to think and watch them disappear. Thoughts disappear into the dharmadhatu.*

Commentary

This is a semdzin that combines the use of the long HŪNG (HŪNG *ring*) and the short HŪNG (HŪNG *thung*), using the enunciated sound of short HŪNGs. 'Long' and 'short' refer to the length of the exhalation and thus the sound. The form and colour of the short HŪNG is irrelevant in this semdzin. This exercise is to be included in a lengthy period of sitting meditation, half an hour, for example, or for a complete meditation session.

We begin the practice by sounding the long HŪNG on the out-breath, mixing the sound with the breath or, to say it another way, projecting the HŪNG on to the breath. When we become distracted by thought trains, then we use the short HŪNG in a staccato sound to dissolve the thoughts and break the flow.

We have used long unsounded HŪNGs mixed with the out-breath in the ngondro. In this exercise, used in tandem with long-sounded HŪNGs we use short-sounded HŪNGs.

If one will do, then definitely do not use two, and if one is good, then it should be enough.

Another way to say it: the long HŪNG is peaceful and the short is wrathful, and the long HŪNG is concentrated and the short one is explosive and destructive. But this long HŪNG recitation is something you can carry around with you, you can do it all day. I mean, you can mutter it under your breath, or you can even do it in silence—it is better to have the gross vibration, though.

So, there is the semdzin of the long and the short HŪNGs—maybe the most valuable of the lot.

Incidentally, the short HŪNG is the mantra of Dorje Trollo. Use it sparingly. Use the long HŪNG as much as possible. Use the short HŪNG infrequently or it will cease to function. The short HŪNG, the PHAT and the HA, these syllables will lose their power if they become too familiar—familiarity breeds contempt.

'Mix your mind with the sound', and as in the ngondro, we have the visualization to concentrate upon, to keep the mind alert while it is pacified. Mixing the mind with the sound and the sound with the breath, and that will keep us from going to sleep. This semdzin is not a pacifier; that's not the purpose of the exercise. The purpose of the exercise is focus.

1/6 The Semdzin of the Syllable RAM

De bzhin du lte bar RAM bsgom la rlung dang lus gnas bstun pa dang

Visualize the syllable RAM in the navel (gut) centre; identify energy (breath) and body in the same place.

CNN: This is navel centre integration, also original chakra (first on the three-channel line). Visualize red RAM in the navel, then sound it softly, fixate on it. Heat arises.

Commentary
Now, the semdzin of the syllable RAM: RAM is the seed syllable of the element fire and naturally it is red in colour. It is presented by Longchemba seemingly as an auxiliary semdzin, one that can be used to create heat in the bodymind in a greater yoga. It can be considered a preliminary practice for tumo, the yoga of the mystic fire, for instance; and it can also be practised as the source of sensory bliss as a door into equanimity. It is important and it is also quite simple.

First visualize the fire-engine red syllable in the navel centre, the solar-plexus, on, or in, the central meridian. This is the centre of integration and the source of activity. Visualize the form of the syllable and its bright radiant translucent red colour. Visualize it glowing and then burning, glowing and burning. Do not take the fire higher than the heart centre. Fixate on the syllable. Sound the syllable softly—rolling the *r* —as you visualize it.

There is no alternative here to visualizing the Tibetan form of the syllable. It is not a complex visualization. If we were to transliterate it, it is comprised of three letters in the roman alphabet, R, A and M. But that combination is clumsy. The Tibetan syllable is about the size of a joint of the thumb.

The syllable of fire is used to generate heat. As such, it is a subsidiary semdzin. It can be used to heat the body when it is cold, or to put heat into the knees, for example, when they are painful. It can be used spontaneously, when we are so inspired. Practised systematically in a larger discipline, we use it in the context of tumo yoga, in the anuyoga context. If we can develop it to the point where it produces heat, or, most significantly, if we can develop it so that we can visualize the syllable in the knees when we have sitting problems, then we make practical use of it.

The visualization and focus can actually generate the physical heat that we require, for example, to melt the snow to a five-meter radius away from the body. But its principal use is in warming the subtle body by visualizing the syllable in the stomach, in the navel centre, visualizing the syllable and the colour. Remember the symbology of the colour red, and the signs of some success in this semdzin is the strong sensation, and ultimately the experience of sensation, of sunyata. Experience 'the burning and the melting'.

The heat that the syllable RAM generates becomes tactile sensation, which in turn becomes the empty bliss of sexual union. Physical heat is the basis of the intensive feeling that is sublimated as 'delight', 'pleasure' or 'bliss'. Focus on the heat as it rises and 'empty delight' or 'pure pleasure' is the product. Explore the connection between heat and sensation, sensation and bliss. Always watch the emptiness of sensation.

Further, by extension, this semdzin can be applied to the yoga of healing. Tibetan medicine attributes all kinds of aches and pains to temperature imbalance—heat or cold. In meditation we need heat in the knees. When muscles and joints are paralysed through cold, they need heat to reinvigorate again. When our knees give us pain we can then automatically warm them. But there may be a lack of heat because of the wide extension of the joint, or simply a lack of heat relative to the rest of the body, or the sinews might be stretched and require heat to relax them. It is an absence of heat in the joints that generally creates pain, and we can focus the RAM in our knees in order to create the heat that warms up the joints and alleviates the pain. The semdzin of the syllable RAM can be highly effective in these cases.

1/7 The Semdzin of Vajrasattva's Body

Lha'i skur bsgom la sna rtse dang ba spu sgo nas sku phra mo 'phro 'du byed pa la sems gtad pas shes pa gsal dag chen po'i nyams skye'o.

Visualize yourself as Vajrasattva and from the tip of the nose and in the hair follicles practice emanation and reabsorption of tiny Vajrasattvas, and with an attentive mind the experience of cognition as magnificent pure luminosity arises.

CNN: i): Visualize yourself as Vajrasattva. b) Visualize Vajrasattva on the tip of the nose, mix the visualization with the out-breath and in breath (as in the first semdzin), remain with empty lungs for an instant. iii) Visualize an infinite number of Vajrasattvas emanating from the pores of the skin and body orifices on the out-breath and returning on the in-breath.

Commentary

The semdzin of the deity's body requires visualization of Vajrasattva (Dorje Sempa). 'Adamantine Being' is a translation of Vajrasattva. 'Dorje' is the name of the ritual instrument and the reality that it represents, which is *rikpa*. 'Sempa' means 'being', as in 'human being' or more specifically as in 'bodhisattva', where it means 'buddha-hero'. In the five-buddha mandala he belongs to the vajra-family of the east.

Vajrasattva is white, which indicates the colour of crystal—crystal clear, translucent. He represents the sambhogakaya form of the lama, the mahaguru, and he holds the vajra and the bell. The vajra standing upright in his right hand at his heart centre, and the bell turned upwards towards his navel in his left hand on his knee. These are symbols of male and female principles, of skilful means and perfect insight (wisdom). Insofar as Vajrasattva is 50% male and 50% female, his body is shown androgynously, the curves are female, and breasts strongly delineated, which is of course true of all bodhisattvas in this sambhogakaya realm. He is androgynous, asexual. He wears silks over his shoulders and around his waist. He wears the bodhisattva's jewel ornaments, and hair knot.

He wears a girdle and jewel ornaments. His crown with the five jewels represents the five wisdoms. A hair ornament holds the hairknot, the yogi's hairpiece, in place. Crown, crest jewel, earrings, short necklace, long necklace, bracelets armlets and anklets comprise the bodhisattva's jewellery. The long necklace may have a double chain. He has a girdle to hold his silken lungi. Regarding the bell, the handle of it is half-vajra, and the bottom part is the bell and clanger. It is held with the bell uppermost.

He has a smiling, somewhat enigmatic face; he sits in lotus

posture. We visualize ourselves in his form. Perhaps the most important part of this visualization is his translucent whiteness. Only silks and jewels cover his nakedness. This all belongs to the symbology of the sambhogakaya. It is a visionary body. And, as we affirm in the refuge prayer, the sambhogakaya is luminosity, it is clarity and that is the nature of his being. The elements of the visualization with which we are identifying—necklaces, crown, earrings, bracelets, anklets and armlets, the ornaments and the belt—symbolize his bodhisattva qualities.

The semdzin begins with the identification of our bodies with the body of Vajrasattva. The colour is the primary element of the visualization upon which to focus. The posture and gesture define the shape; the principal symbols are vajra and bell. So first visualize yourself as Vajrasattva. Visualize your body like translucent crystal. Visualize the lotus posture, and visualize the right hand at the heart, holding the vajra upright, and the left hand on the knee holding the bell.

The second stage of the visualization is the small Vajrasattva at the end of the nose. Mix that visualization with the breath; visualize the projection and retraction of the small Vajrasattva along with the out-breath and the in-breath.

Thirdly visualize tiny Vajrasattvas in all the apertures of the body—the ears, eyes, nostrils, mouth, breasts, genitals and anus—and also in every pore, and hair follicle, of the skin. Then with deep breathing we keep the Vajrasattva on the tip of the nose projecting and retracting, and at the same time we visualize the entire body breathing through its apertures and pores. Visualize stale air, the waste energy of the bodymind, being ejected through all the pores and apertures of the body. As we breathe in, we breathe in the prana through those same apertures. So, our entire body is breathing, but it is breathing with the mind. The mind is breathing.

Finally, we visualize the Vajrasattvas in all the apertures and pores of the body moving out from their lodging on the out-breath and back into their home on the in-breath. The Vajrasattvas in the orifices and the pores are projected out on the exhalation and retire on the inhalation. We are Vajrasattva, the one Vajrasattva is doing this, and then millions of Vajrasattvas are doing it. This is projection and reabsorption. The body is breathing in a way, and so is the mind breathing.

Second Series: Freedom from Attachment

Gnyis pa lus sems 'dzin zhen dpral ba'i gnad bdun ni rlung dang gnad sdar bzhin la

Through the second sevenfold series cloying attachment is flayed from the body and mind.

CNN: Overcoming attachment to body and mind and concepts.

NB: The second series strips away attachment to body, speech and mind. It deals with energy, with prana [*tsalung*]. We do not have a precise word for the translation of *prana*, though 'energy' is adequate. Certainly 'wind' or 'air' or other various aspects of prana are inappropriate.

2/1 The Semdzin of the Pink Pearl Between the Eyes

Smin mtsham su thig le dkar dmar 'dres pa sran ma'i ga'u tsam la sems gzung ngo. Des rlung gi nyams skye'o

Focus the mind on a white/red sphere the size of a pea between the eye brows. Experiences of energy arises thereby.

CNN: The sphere is pink; solar and lunar united. Prana concentrates at the point of mental focus. Concentrate sharply/intensively; relax into the state.

Commentary

The instruction on the semdzin of the pink pearl is very simple. Between the eye brows, or slightly above, is the place of the *urna*, which is the protuberant mark on the forehead of buddha-icons. It is one of the thirty-five marks of the buddha— physical marks. On the physical level, behind this mark are the pituitary gland and the head chakra. Try to feel or imagine the external spot; there may be a slight depression in the forehead. Find the place, tap it with the middle finger of the right hand and produce a sensation there. Now visualize a globe, a bubble, a small sphere on that spot. It is the size of a pearl in a pearl necklace, slightly smaller than a pea. Its colour is very important; it is a mixture of red and white—variegated red and white, or pink. It is the same colour as Guru Rinpoche's facial complexion. It can be visualized as pink like a pink pearl. Simply focus on that sphere, on the spot between the eyebrows. Perhaps there will be a tingling where it touches. We need intensive, fixated concentration to begin with to identify the sphere and to isolate it. Then after we have it fixed, we can relax a bit with our attention in the sphere. Then finally relax completely. Keep the concentration in the sphere and when we know we are about to lose it, relax completely as it happens. And we can move the level of concentration from intense at the beginning, when we are focusing energy and mind on the sphere, to partially relaxed, watching it again, and then, finally, fully relaxed, and we are at the end of the semdzin.

Regarding the spatial and colour symbolism, it is externalized at the level of the head chakra on the central channel meridian; it is the red and white mix of the right and left channels. Furthermore, it is like an externalization of the pituitary gland, which is relevant to Hindus. I do not think it is useful for us to make that identification here.

Wherever we put our mind, energy gathers and concentrates.

That is a fundamental principle of tantra, to be applied when the skilful means aspect dominates and where control is required. This principle applies to our own body, to another's body, or to something in the environment. When mind and energy are united and mind is quiescent, then energy is stilled—simple! So mix the energy with the mind and concentrate it and our energy is brought into equilibrium. We do not have to have that information for the principle to operate. Concentrate on the sphere between the eyebrows as a method of controlling energy. Nervous energy (*rlung*), is the 'air' in the body that creates uncontrolled thought-trains causing emotional imbalance and disease. Tibetan psychiatry is mainly concerned with the movements of this *lung*, the energy within the body.

The sign of success of this concentration exercise in the mixing of the colours—the red and the white—is some elevation in our energy level. This may be experienced as some irritability, excitement, nervousness, increase in mental activity, or some vague feeling in the body.

2/2 The Semdzin of the Three Staffs
or The Semdzin of the Arrow and Noose

Lus kyi dbus na rtsa gum dbyu gu drangs po ltar gnas pa'i ro rkyang gi sna bug na yod pa nas rlung bzung ste mda' ltar 'phangs pas nad gdon sdig sgrib dag zhags pa ltar nang du bkug pas dbu ma'i ma sna nas tshud de rtsa gsum 'khor lo bzhi ye shes kyi rlung gis gang ba la sems bzung bas rig pa stong gsal gyi nyams skye'o

The three channels are like straight staffs at the centre of the body; the *roma* (left) and *kyangma* (right) exit at the nostrils. Inhale and then exhale forcefully like shooting an arrow and illness and disease and faults and errors are eradicated/purified; then inhaling like a lasso catch the prana and bring it into the central

channel through the nose and it will infuse the three channels and the four chakras with awareness.

Focusing on that, the empty clarity of *rikpa* will be experienced.

NB: Staff is yugu (*dbyu gu*).

Commentary

This is the semdzin of the three staffs. A staff is a long shepherd's stick without a crook at the top. The three staffs refer to the three *nadis*—the right, left and central channels of the body of subtle energy. The central channel runs from the fontanel to the perineum. Four fingers below the navel is the junction of the right and left channels with the central channel. At their top end, the right and left channels turn over and join the nostrils. The right channel is white, the left channel is red, and the central channel is blue. The colours may be reversed when the yogi visualizes the dakini and when a yogini visualizes the male yidam.

Breathing out, the breath is like an arrow shot from a bow. When the arrow dissolves at the end of its flight there is a momentary pause. Breathing in, the prana enters the right and left channels and infuses the central channel below the navel. On the in-breath prana is drawn in as if it were caught in a lasso, pulled in through the nostrils, the entrances to the right and left channels, and down to the junction with the central channel, where it moves upwards to invigorate the navel, heart, throat and head chakras.

Here are some associations with the 'three staffs'. Their shape is like a modified trident. In Tibetan the right channel is called *kyangma*; the left channel is called *roma*, and the central channel is called *uma*. The right, *kyangma*, is 'the one and only', 'the only one', 'the single'. The left channel, the *roma* means 'taste', taste as in *rochik*, 'one-taste' for instance. In Tibetan *roma* means *raas*, which is used to describe the variant sensations of the tongue, but also for the 'taste', the feeling tone, of music and of sentiment and emotion. The central channel is, of course, called *uma*, 'the middle one'. The *kyangma* relates to the absolute, the male; the *roma* relates to the relative, the female. The *kyangma* is the cold white moon and the *roma* is the hot red sun—male and female are reversed here. The sun is associated with blood and the moon associated with semen, which is a harmony. And the energy of the right is represented as semen and the left is represented as blood. Right is *yab* and left is *yum* and the centre is *yab-yum*, union. The right represents upaya (*thabs*), male, skilful means, and the left represents prajña (*shes rab*), the female, insight into the nature of all things as emptiness. If you want simpler words for *sherab* and *thab*, then they are wisdom and compassion.

The out-breath, is expelled like an arrow, and the arrow is sent far away, taking with it any indisposition, any kind of sickness, any neurosis, any obstacles in meditation, any negativities whatsoever. And then the in-breath, like a lasso capturing pure prana through the two nostrils, down the right and left channels, pressing it into the central channel below the navel, then that prana, that energy, is rising in the central channel through the navel centre, heart centre, throat centre, to the thousand-petal lotus at the top of the head.

Channels are representations—symbols—of subtle energy flows; there is nothing material or substantial to be found; the channels change size and shape and constellation, and may be reversed in significance.

roma	kyangma	uma
karmic	karmic	pure
red	white	blue
yum	yab	union

mater	pater	hermaphrodite
relative	absolute	unity of relative and absolute
blood	semen	
left	right	
sherab	thab	
energy	visible form	
female	male	
moon	sun	

2/3 Semdzin of the White Sphere

Sna rtser rlung dkar po mda'i gang nas dpag tshad rgyang kyi bar du khug pa gnyis phar song tshur 'ong la sems bzung bas rtog med gsal ba'i nyams skye'o

On the tip of the nose a prana-sphere, carried away like an arrowshot on the exhalation from a metre to a kilometre away and brought back by the inhalation. Focus on this and you will experience radiant nonthought.

NB: See also 1/1 White 'A'. Here the sphere is of *prana (rlung)*.

CNN: Remain empty at the end of the out-breath in order to calm the mind. First breath out to a place near, then further away to places you know, then to foreign places you do not know.

Commentary
This semdzin is like the semdzin of the white 'A'. Visualize a white sphere (*tiklé*) at the end of the nose and then mixing it with the breath project it on the out-breath and retract it on the in-breath. When that function is automatic, send the sphere further away on the out-breath and retract it in the same manner. Send the sphere to different places—into the

garden, into town, to another country, to another continent.

Longchemba says. 'You'll experience brilliant nonthought.'

2/4 Semdzin of the Rainbow Body

Lus byin 'od lnga'i rwa ba 'ja' tshon lta bu sang ma seng khrel ma khrol shags ma gshigs la ma yengs bar sems bzung bas 'od gsal dag pa'i nyams skye'o

Focus unwaveringly on your transfigured body [*byin*] as a [net] of five coloured light, translucent and clear like a rainbow, bright and shining, and you will experience the pure clear light.

NB: Is the rainbow light distinct from the clear light?

CNN: Visualize the white letter 'A' at the centre of the body, articulate the sound 'A', and visualize rays of light emanating in all directions.

Commentary
Visualize the body sitting in lotus posture in a sphere that touches both fontanel and perineum and visualize a small shining white letter 'A' at the heart centre. The heart centre is half way between the perineum and the fontanel on the central channel; it is the centre of the bodymind and the centre of the globe that we are visualizing. Visualize rays of five coloured light emanating out of the white 'A', globally, in all directions simultaneously, limited only by the globe. The five colours of the rainbow are red, yellow, green, blue and white. The rainbow light emanates continuously and it is soft-coloured light and radiant.

We visualize light moving from the centre to the circumference, in the entirety of the sphere in a 360-degree global movement. The vision we have here is of our bodymind as light. We can obtain the vision of our body as clear light during the visualization or when we cease the visualization. Articulation of the 'A' is best done silently. This is a dematerialization exercise.

2/5 The Semdzin of Transference

Rlung sems nam mkha'i mthongs su 'phangs nas yi ge'am 'od kyi gong bu'am nyi zla'i dkyil 'khor je mtho je mtho las mthar dbyings su nub nas bltar mi mngon pa'i ngang la sems bzung bas stong nyid bsam mno dang bral 'ba'i nyams skye'o

Focus on the spirit ['energy' and the 'rational mind'] shot into space as a letter, a ball of light or a sun and moon sphere, moving higher and higher into the sky until it vanishes altogether. You experience emptiness beyond mentation/thought.

CNN: The letters you may use are the glottal 'A' *or* HŪNG. *Alternative to transference: unify everything, internal and external into the glottal* 'A' *or tiklé - all phenomena, all experience, body, speech and mind; the* 'A' *or tiklé then vanishes.*

Commentary

On the top of the head at the fontanel, visualize an empty sphere of light like a bubble. Put the entire universe inside this sphere: all mind and all energy; all external and all internal phenomena, the subjective knower, and the external field of phenomenal appearances; the grasper and the grasped and the grasping; all thought and concepts whatsoever; all feeling and emotion. Add the five skandhas: name and form; positive, neutral, negative reaction; concepts; propensities (*samskaras*); and the eight types of consciousness. Add the five elements: earth, water, fire, air and space. Add all sentient beings and all buddhas. To include all and everything whatsoever, we may put the subjective knower and all objective appearances represented by the right and the left channels, the red and the white, into the sphere. The contents of the bodymind is emptied into the sphere, or to say it another way, we are turned inside out into the sphere. Then set off the bubble like a rocket with the assistance of the articulated sound HŪNG, the sphere rises from the top of the head and climbs into the sky, rising faster and faster until it is shot into the stratosphere. Finally, it bursts open and its contents dissolve into pure space.

We are turning ourselves inside out. Just turn your outside in, so that you are inside that bubble while outside is space. But there is no one remaining to send the bubble out into space!

The sphere is blown away, like shot into space, and it just slowly, slowly, vanishes until it is completely gone. This is dissolution into space.

Through the syllable RAM there is dissolution by fire. Visualize the moments of death: the elements—earth, water, fire, air and space, respectively—are dissolving and we have visions of the cataclysmic elements, earthquake relating to earth, flood and tsunami relating to water, conflagration and firestorm relating to fire, and then finally wind, the stormy gale. There is a grand finale related to each of the elements. Here in the semdzin of transference, it is the one relating to space. As in all these semdzins, finally, what we are doing is unifying duality. It is best not to look for rational descriptions or explanations.

2/6 The Semdzin of Ear Consciousness

Sems rna ba la gtad de lhan ne bzung bas sgra'i bsam gtan gyi nyams skye'o.

Focus attention in the ear, relax, and you will experience the samadhi of (absorption in) sound.

CNN: Fixate on sound not the source of sound, fixate on hearing, put consciousness inside the ear, relax body and mind. In the samadhi of sound (nyam) hear auditory visions, sounds, voices, words, also the languages of animals and birds, talk with unseen beings.

Commentary

This semdzin is simply the semdzin of sound. Bring consciousness back from the source of the sound and keep it in the ear. As a prop, use the internal sound of the inner ear that may resound like the syllable OM (or tintinnabulation) to focus the sound in the ear. Press the ear to enliven an inner sound. Alternatively, we can visualize a tiny bodhisattva Chenresik (the four-armed Avalokiteśvara) in the inner ear. Chenresik is the bodhisattva of ear consciousness, the bodhisattva of the western direction, and also of our aeon. We fixate out attention in the ear but not upon any single sound, allowing whatever sound arising to pass without judgement or projection as in non-judgmental or mirror-like listening. Thus, the practice is a combined concentration/awareness (shamatā/ vipasyana) exercise.

Confirm that consciousness habitually flies to the object of the sound, the source of the sound. It does this through the natural propensity to attachment and to locate the sound in a specific place in the environment. Reflect also upon the way an emotional response arises with the sound. Listening too closely and hearing with attachment provokes anger or delight, for example, in response to the noises other people or other generators make. If we defocus the listening we do not hear the insult.

2/7 The Semdzin of Vajrasattva in the Heart Centre

Snying ngang du lha sku phra mo la sems bzung bas 'od gsal dag pa'i nyams skye zhing bar do'i 'od gsal 'byongs ba dang lha'i sku ring bsrel 'ja 'od 'byung ba'o

By focusing on (or putting your mind into) a tiny body of Samantabhadra in your heart centre you will experience pure clear light and attaining the clear light of the bardo at death there will be buddha-deity, ringsel and rainbow light.

CNN: Visualize Samantabhadra or Vajrasattva: concentrate fixedly then relax.

Commentary.

In the heart centre, visualize a tiny blue sphere, perhaps 3mm (1/8") in diameter, and in that sphere sits a tiny Samantabhadra, the Adi-buddha, the original all-embracing buddha, the first buddha, the buddha behind every mandala. He represents the natural state of being and awareness. The representation of Samantabhadra, the All-Good Buddha holds his legs in lotus posture (*vajrasan*) and hands in meditation gesture (*dhyana mudra*). His colour is blue, translucent blue. He wears no silks or jewels. He is the naked, blue buddha. The form is semi-symmetrical. Concentrate fixedly, fully and attentively on Samantabhadra and the body becomes a body of light. Then completely relax and forget it. Do this only occasionally. Do not allow it to become a habit or an obsession.

All moments of experience of the here and now are equal and this Samantabhadra semdzin is the ultimate guarantor that there can be no moment that is fundamentally different. Thus, Samantabhadra allows us to slip through the moment of death and into the clear light experience—which is no other than himself—and then perhaps through the option of emanation of the mandalas of the five buddhas, and then through the experiences of potential location of conception, and the place of choosing father and mother, and so on, and then into the womb and out the other side.

Thus this semdzin is particularly useful as preparation for crossing the bardo—the in-between spaces—when required. It is useful when crossing the bardo of the moment of death, the bardo of clear light, the bardo of reality, and then the bardo of rebirth: these four bardos.

The seed of the semdzin comes to fruition at the moment of death, and we float through the chasms of radical change in empty light. It takes care of the bardos of dying and rebirth and it also takes care of every conceivable change in this lifetime.

This semdzin promises utmost efficacy and somehow shows exactly what a semdzin is and what it should do. It functions on a level quite beyond concepts.

Remember the nature of the heart centre—all-embracing empty spaciousness. The syllable that represents it is the HŪNG, the blue HŪNG: the nature of the heart centre that is emptiness, spaciousness and light.

As an adjunct and support to this semdzin take a small printed icon of Samantabhadra, fold it up into a tiny ball, and secrete it in an amulet, or in a gau (a small metal box, a portable shrine), or inside a statue of a buddha or a buddha-deity.

What we are asked to do in this semdzin of Samantabhadra is to focus on the central point of the body. It is actually a point instant, and has no particular place of rest; it has no dimension, but symbolically it is sesame-sized This is a very powerful exercise, and Longchemba thought so also, because he recommended it as the semdzin that will take us through the bardos of death and rebirth. As an exercise for preparation for death it is second to none. The best use of the thought of death is to keep us totally in the here and now and thus the old axiom that defines the primary motivation for the mahayana and tantric practices—'All yoga is preparation for death'. In this context 'yoga' means any kind of spiritual exercise or meditation.

Of course, concern with death is an outlying ornament in the Dzogchen mandala. We have no issues with the bardos; all Dzogchen practice already defines and transcends the bardos. Every moment of existence is the penetration of the bardos. It is done in the moment. There is going to be no difference between this moment and any moment in the dying and rebirth process. And this yoga, this Samantabhadra semdzin is our guarantee of that.

Longchemba also promises residual *ringsel* after death. Ringsel, exoterically, indicates 'relics'. When a Dzogchen lama leaves in rainbow body, he will leave ringsel behind. Usually he will leave hair and toe and fingernails and teeth, too. But that's not mentioned by Longchemba in his text.

Be sure, it is the semdzin of Samantabhadra that produces rainbow body with ringsel as evidence. And again, it is very much a matter of an intense period of practice, illuminating the 'A', recognizing Samantabhadra in the heart centre, which, having been identified and substantiated, as it were, thereafter needs only an occasional recognition to sustain the reality, his power.

To merely think of it is the beginning of the process, but if we think about it, then we cannot do anything else—can we? If we remember it as thought, then our mind is full of remembrances, which obviously is not the here and now—is it?

Keeping Samantabhadra in the heart centre requires no

practice at all—nonmeditation, nonaction, nonconduct. Once it has been located, it stays where it has always been. No activity of the rational mind will make any difference. Recall of the awareness or presence of *rikpa* is the only sign of its activation.

What about that Zen story about the two monks traveling together. They come to a river bank and find a beautiful girl waiting there. She asks for a lift to the other side. The elder immediately takes her on his back and crosses the river and lets her down on the other bank. The two monks leave her there and continue on for some time, and finally the young one says:

'You shouldn't have done that!'

'What shouldn't I have done?' asks the elder.

'You shouldn't have carried that girl on your back, or even touched her. It is forbidden.'

'Ah, the girl!' the other replies. 'I left her by the river. Why do you still carry her with you?'

This anecdote illustrates how the superior SAMAYA supersedes the lesser; but of greater practical significance, it shows the folly of adhesive thought-trains.

The Third Series: Revealing The Nature of Mind

Gsum pas chos nyid mthong ba bstan pa'i bdun tshan ni

The third series of seven parts reveals the nature of mind.

NB: Nature of mind: reality (*dharmata, chos nyid, stong pa nyid*).

CNN: The nature of mind is our natural condition or state.

Commentary
Now the third series is rather different from the first two series. We discuss the concepts involved in the third series while talking about Dzogchen practice. But here we have them listed in a very useful way. It serves as a memory device, to have all the twenty-one semdzins in three series, and particularly in this third series, because they are what we could call mind-semdzins. Of course, all semdzins are mind-semdzins, but here we will see that 'mind' has a particular meaning.

The first two of the third series of seven deal with meditation on emptiness. 'Through this third series of seven, the nature of mind is revealed'. The first series leads to quiescence, to a peaceful place. The second flays attachment from the bodymind. The third gives us recognition of the nature of mind. Recognition of the nature of mind is initiatory, of course, and it is, thereafter, supportive to memory of initiation, of initiatory experience.

3/1 The Semdzin of The Gradual Revelation of Emptiness

Stong nyid rim gyis pa la sems gzung ba ni dang por bsil la ming du ma la sogs pas gzhigs te mgo gcig bu la'ang ming du mas bsil la ming de don la brtag pas don rdul phran du song dus ming gang na 'dug btsal bas ma rnyed pa'i tshe gang yang yid la rgyu ba'i stong nyid phugs rdugs su shar ba'i ngang la 'tshol khro dang dran bsam med par lhan ne bzhag pas stong pa gnyis su med pa'i nyams skye'o. Lus ji lta ba bzhin snang ba thams cad la sbyar ro.

The semdzin of graduated emptiness [*stong-nyid rim-gyis-pa*]: Firstly, fragmentation, analysis by name etc: our one head (for example) is composed of many named parts and by examining the meaning of the name it is broken down into atomic parts, and then searching for what is meant by the name nothing is found and in the consequent space of ultimately undone emptiness in the mind and by relaxing without analysing and without any mentation the experience of nondual emptiness arises. In the same way that this method is applied to body it can be applied to all phenomena (appearances).

NB: This is the sutra method: See Mipham, *Calm and Clear* for expansive detail. Chokyi Nyima Rinpoche recurrently demonstrates this method: 'Gaze at your neighbour's face—what does 'face' imply?'

CNN: First appraise the subject: 'Where is the 'I?' In the madhyamika view the 'I' is an aggregation. Then appraise the object: 'What is concrete? What is substantial?' Finally consider 'phenomenal emptiness' (*snang-stong*).

As evidence: fixate on a pain in your body, analyse and 'see' the emptiness. Consider the pain in your knees: if your empty concentration is strong enough the pain will dissolve.

Commentary

The first of the seven semdzins revealing the nature of mind is the semdzin of graduated emptiness, or rather the graduated discovery of emptiness. This is achieved through the mahayana practice of discursive analysis of the psycho-organism and the eventual discovery of its nature as emptiness.

There are two gradualistic ways to approach emptiness, two ways to arrive at the certainty of emptiness. One is through the madhyamika philosophical analysis that has implicit within it a dialectic that leaves us in a place in which only emptiness can be experienced. For a particular kind of logical mind that method is eminently functional. The second is an existential analysis of the psycho-organism. Either way, it is a slow process. In the first one, we need to study madhyamika philosophy, and this can take one or several lifetimes. The examination of the psycho-organism, on the other hand, takes a matter of minutes in a graduated process of discursive meditation, but needs constant repetition.

The method of analysis of the body-mind, the psycho-organism, is done in the psychological academies of Buddhism, but more significantly it is done in the laboratory of the mind. It is this latter method that we will focus on now.

If there is nothing substantial in the body-mind, if there is nothing there that is a constant in all our experience, and, if you like, through past and future lives, then there is nothing, and that nothing is emptiness. So the meditation is to focus on the body-mind, and analyse it with the tools of the tradition and attempt to discover something concrete. We can pose the problem as: 'Who or what is the 'I'?'. We can make it more direct: 'Who am I?'. So, in this analysis, we start with the name. You call me Joe, you call me Joe Bloggs.

But when you look at what is there, then the name refers to the sum of many parts. If I am what you see here, this form, then the form again is the sum of parts. There is nothing called 'the body', the body actually is an aggregate of limbs and torso, head and physical sense organs, etc. Well, if 'I' am not the body and not the name, then maybe I am the mind. 'I' am something alive inside the body? 'I' am what survives death? What survives death? It is called the 'principle of consciousness.' 'I' am consciousness? So, in this analysis we attempt to focus on what is consciousness. Stand behind the consciousness and watch it and see what it is exactly. And all we find is a series of sensory perceptions. We know that these sensory perceptions are transient because they are always in the present and the present is always passing, changing; perception of the present is by definition ephemeral. Is there actually an essence of consciousness that retains constancy through every perception? In the laboratory of the mind, check it out, see if such a thing can be isolated. Can you locate anything? Does 'I' have any extension in time from birth to death? Surely this 'principle of consciousness' refers to a constant personality, or constant propensities to act or to think in certain ways. Well, it certainly changed from childhood to adolescence, to manhood, to maturity, to old age. I think of myself as a person, as something constant, but when I come to examine it, there is only a changing identity—nothing constant. This 'I' is an ego constituted of constant, persistent, projections—projections meaning self-images. But then again, searching for it, what we find in this personality is only constant change. 'I' am a succession of emotional states or sentiments, something that is totally reactive, reflexively reactive, something which responds to the environment, constantly changing as the environment changes. So what is the 'I'? And who are we as individuals?

Let's go back to this principle of consciousness again. Let's consider the 'soul'. Maybe this is the fundamental personality or the basis of the 'I'. But what are its constituents, what are its qualities, and if these qualities and constituents have any substance, what and where is it that retains a constancy through our life? Let's isolate this supposed entity. If it exists, then surely it should be perceived or intuited or in some way made aware in the examination of the psyche in meditation. Or maybe the soul is, again, a useful concept that we have come to believe in as something substantial, a concept that produces a product, a virtuous expedient product, that actually has no existence. And again, the principle of consciousness: if this principle of consciousness actually exists, then where does it exist? In which part of the body does it lodge? If we cut off our limbs, then this principle of consciousness still exists? You let surgeons take out your heart in an operation, do you lose your principle of consciousness in the process? Where is this consciousness lodged?

Like this, we analyse our body-mind down to nothing. Introduce the physicist's evidence: What is the nature of the cell, the atom, the quark? Nothing essential can be found. Again, what we're left with is emptiness, which we can define provisionally as the absence of anything substantial or quantifiable. We could also define it usefully as the principle of change: popular wisdom has it, 'Nothing is constant except change!'—somewhat nihilistic?!

The meditation is to find the 'I'. We are looking for the personality, or rather the essential, substantial part of the personality. If we perform this meditation conclusively, then we arrive at the space of emptiness. We have convinced ourselves of the illogicality of anything but emptiness, and we've proved to ourselves experientially that there's nothing that we experience in the psyche that has any substance. We know only that change is constant, that 'reality' is in constant flux, and underneath that or within that or permeating that, flux is emptiness. That is the first semdzin of the third series. It's a discursive meditation, which in Mahayana Buddhism is a common form of meditation. In Vajrayana or in Tantra and in Dzogchen discursive meditation is generally discouraged. In Dzogchen, it may be considered counter-productive. In Vajrayana, the discursive meditations are this discursive meditation on emptiness or the nature of 'I', the discursive meditation on impermanence, discursive meditation on suffering. There is a discursive meditation on the precious human body, in which the great blessing of this human situation is contemplated. There are meditations on the four boundless qualities—equanimity, loving kindness, compassion and sympathetic joy. There are others.

In this graduated process of discovering emptiness, we are looking for a substantial, permanent aspect of the body-mind, or personality. Perhaps the most efficient method is to work through the five skandhas (or aggregates) which subsume all the elements of our experience: first we look at name and form that provide the first level of experience, then the quality of our instinctual responses, the concepts that define them, the sensory and emotional associations that arise and finally the consciousness that illuminates. Arriving at the certainty of an absence of anything substantial or permanent, we are resting the mind in resultant emptiness.

3/2 The Semdzin of Immediate Emptiness

Stong nyid cig car ba la sems bzung ba ni: ci snang la cher gyis btlas dus stong sangs sangs song ba bsams la gzugs snang sgra snang la sogs pa thams cad la sbyangs pas snang ba thams cad me long la has btab pa lta bu'i nyams skye'o.

The semdzin of immediate emptiness: Gaze intently at whatever appears and regard it [visualize it, think of it] as utterly pure and empty. Applying this to all forms and all sounds etc, and all appearances are

experienced like condensation on a mirror.

NB: Synonyms: immediate, direct, instantaneous (*cig car ba*).

CNN: This is the function of self-liberation, natural liberation (rang grol): gaze intently at the nature of any sensory image or perception and it vanishes into emptiness.

Commentary

The second approach to emptiness is through the semdzin of direct or immediate emptiness which is instantaneous experience in which the intellect is sidelined. This is done by a fixed gaze at whatever arises in the fields of consciousness.

This semdzin is practised as an auxiliary exercise in the mainstream of simply sitting, abiding in the natural space, the main Dzogchen practice. The instruction here is simply to fix whatever arises with a penetrating gaze that looks directly into it and perceives the emptiness of appearances immediately. Evidently, here is reason why the eyes remain open during Dzogchen meditation—we can use the field of visionary appearances, eyes wide open. We can also use the sphere of sound, fixing on whatever arises in the ear—compare this exercise with the semdzin of sound. And we can use the other senses, too, taste and touch and smell, which is rather more difficult, because our consciousness in those sensory fields is less developed. Let's leave the tongue and the nose out of it, but include the tactile sense of the skin—remember the pain in your knees in meditation. The skin is difficult to focus upon but there are moments, particularly of pain, that focus our consciousness in an area of the skin or the flesh that allows us perfect practice of this fixed 'gaze'. The 'gaze' here is the gaze of consciousness into the physical pain, or into any focus of pain whatsoever. But focus on pain is simply an example of the fixed gaze of consciousness at an object in a sensory field. A 'gaze' is a fixed focus of consciousness.

This semdzin of direct, immediate, emptiness is of vital importance. If we do not have experience with emptiness, if we have not had the spontaneous arising of an experience of emptiness, if we haven't had an initiatory experience, and we do not know what it is, experientially, then this is a very good way into it.

Another point here is that if we gaze at any sensory object whatsoever long enough it will eventually vanish. Vanish into what? If it is a thought, what does every thought vanish into?

3/3 The Semdzin of Impermanence

Mi rtag pa la sems gzung ba ni: snang ba btad med du sbyong ba ste. Gang snang gtad pa med bden pa med sna tshogs su snang bas mi bden te ris med du 'gyur la mi rtag pa'i phir snyam du sbyongs pas gza' gtad dang bral ba'i nyams skye'o

The semdzin of impermanence: Cultivating appearances as uncertain, undependable, variable [*gtad med du*]: Whatever arises, appearing in a variable and non-veridical variety, becomes a delusion (a lie) and indeterminate; training yourself to think that it is because of impermanence, experience of freedom from grasping arises.

NB: Think conventional time; Think 'change and decay'; Know that all creatures are born to die, suddenly and alone; Know that all forms of life go through changes; Look at the transience of the fabric of existence; Think - the nature of time – illusion; Watch change.

CNN: Beyond mental commitment, freed from grasping (gza' gtad dang bral ba), catch yourself in judgement (of others, of oneself, of phenomena) positive or negative, and think 'this changes from one moment to the next, so any judgment is futile'.

Commentary

The third of the semdzins of revelation of the nature of mind is the semdzin of impermanence. This has both experiential and discursive aspects.

The external preliminary vajrayana meditation of the four mind changes (*blo 'das rnam pa bzhi*) includes the discursive meditation on impermanence and is a corollary of this semdzin and can be included in it.

The experiential method is simple and too easy. This is watching the nature of mind in the experiential flow and perceiving that it exists only as the present. The future never comes and the past never existed. To live our lives as if the future is going to come, and by and through that thought substantiating it, and by creating the past as memory and thus believing in its existence, substantiating past and future, we overlook the reality that only exists in the present.

Accepting the present entirely, we exist in the timeless moment, which can never be perceived as an 'I' conscious of an other. That timeless moment which can never be objectified is *rikpa*, awareness. We can know it only as *rikpa* because the very present cannot be perceived dualistically. The present is never graspable, because the thought by which we conceive it is always a moment later—too late! This is impermanence known experientially. Nothing exists: everything we 'know' is subsumed under the delusory rubric of past, present and future. The future never comes, the past has gone, the present is never graspable. This is change.

The practice of this semdzin is to watch change. The analysis is so simple it is absurd, but ignorance of its meaning traps us in the cage of samsara, the cage of dualistic disjunction. On the contrary, by subsisting on this level of perfect understanding of impermanence, *rikpa* naturally arises and we find ourselves in that spaciousness where lies perfect synchronicity of awareness with being. Identifying with the conceptual generalizations that arise from the belief in the permanence of the elements of existence we are denied the possibility of recognizing *rikpa*.

If the mind is sluggish and impermanence is unrecognisable, or if the mind is overexcited and agitated, then fall back on the discursive aspect of this semdzin, which is the discursive iteration of the fact of gross and inevitable change: everybody dies; there is no escape from death; there may be longevity, but there is no eternal life; we never know when death will overtake us; we never know whether we are going to wake up in the morning; we can never foresee the moment of death. And the other associated thoughts: death is the dissolution of all experience, it is a very painful condition in that we cannot take anything with us to help us, that we leave all our friends and loved ones behind, that we die alone. Then we remember the friends who are of advanced age and those who have died recently, in the past week or year, events that we tend to put out of mind.

Apply this regular dose of discursive understanding to the meditation on impermanence: it concerns the implications of judgement and discrimination. Insofar as we never have the same thing happening in two successive moments, insofar as no moment of experience can be replicated, any judgement that we make is valid only for a split second of experience. Any generalization that we make based upon that judgement, a judgement that depends upon circumstances never to be repeated, is a judgement without much validity. The sense of self is constructed out of such arbitrary and suspect judgements.

Spend five minutes to an hour on this, recognizing that we cannot force understanding of impermanence, but that what we are doing is always done in the present and that there is nothing that we can do to avoid it. We remain totally in the present, identifying with the change, never letting a second moment arise—always keeping with the first moment, the first, pristine, moment of experience.

One last thought concerning this semdzin: the practice is designed to release the very attachments that obsess us—like food, clothing, shelter and sex—and thereby inhibit their attainment. Free from such attachment (and negative attachment) in the spontaneity of the pure and natural state, all things may be granted to us.

3/4 The Semdzin of the Five Great Elements

'Byung ba lnga gang snang gi steng du shes pa tshe ne tshe ne ma yengs par bzhag pas bzhag sa der grol ba'i nyams su myong ba rmi lam dang 'dra ba skye'o.

Focus consciousness unwaveringly, without any distraction upon whatever of the five elements appears, and you will experience self-liberation in that place of focus like dream experience.

Commentary
The five elements are the five great elements: earth, water, fire, air and space. We know them as they appear in nature: earth appears as earth or rock or soil; water appears as the ocean, in a river or stream, in a pond or a vessel, or as rain; fire appears burning as an initial spark, a blazing fire or as glowing embers; air appears as the movement of air or wind; and space appears as expansiveness. The focus on the nature of the elements may resolve into a meditation upon their sound: the sound of the earth when applying an ear to the

soil, the sound of pieces of wood knocking together, the slapping of balls of clay; water falling, flowing or dripping; fire ('dakinis' harmonie') crackling, roaring, whooshing, hissing, humming and snapping; the wind in the leaves or the eves, or the sound of a bird's wings. Space is experienced lying supine on your back on the ground exhaling into the expanse of the sky.

The classical analysis of sensory experience according to these five elements—although they have been overtaken by scientific categories—is still highly efficient. It is widely used in Tantra as in Dzogchen. Each of the chakras is related to one of the elements and thereby outer and inner are united.

The semdzin of the five elements is to focus on the elements as they arise in consciousness. This is to be understood as when elements arise in their pure nature (where pure means virtually unmixed). When, adventitiously, we find the five elements in their raw forms, then we can gaze into their nature and this is done with a fixed concentration upon the experience of the moment.

It can also be useful to understand the abstract connotations of the five great elements. Earth implies solidity, a concrete concentration, like landscape, a tree or a flower, and the human body itself. Water implies liquidity, a potential or actual flowing. Fire implies heat or temperature derived from the sun or an external source or within the bodymind. Air implies mobility like the wind and breath itself. Space implies emptiness and whatever is completely unobstructable, like the sky. Solidity, liquidity, heat, mobility and emptiness may seem to be abstract, academic categories, but focussing upon the raw elements, visions characterized by these properties can arise.

Longchemba says that such experience is like dream

experience. Putting attention into the nature of such visionary phenomena—which is nothing other than saying concentrating upon one of the five elements—'Each moment of experience is naturally and reflexively liberated and the nature of mind is realized and the natural state of being is entered into.'

3/5 The Semdzin of Nonthought

Mi rtog pa la sems gzung ba ni snang ba gang snang shes pa ci 'gyus skad cig ma'i phreng ba cha med rtog bral du ye nas gnas pa de ngos bzung la 'jur la thebs par sbyangs pas rtog med rang gnas chen po'i bsam gtan skye'o

The semdzin of nonthought: Whatever appearance arises in consciousness, whatever moves in the necklace-sequence of instants, intuitively apprehend its indivisible, thoughtfree ultimate nature. Holding the mind in this way [*'jur la thebs pa*] the samadhi of intrinsical nonthought arises.

NB: Nonthought (*mi rtog pa*), like the silence within sound, is the emptiness of thought. Meditation on time entails recognition of instants inseparable from consciousness of sensory impression or, to say it another way, watching the nature of mind.

Commentary
When direct sensory perception arises free of filtration by the rational mind—free of apperception—the mind is thoughtfree. The method is simply to focus upon appearances—upon lightform—external, internal or unitary, as they arise, and look into their empty radiant nature. The focus and awareness are automatic functions. If the thinker objectifies thoughts in a process of identification, then there will be no relaxing into the nature of the thought, the thoughtless space within.

Nonthought cannot be defined usefully as the gap between thoughts or the empty space inside the thought or the space in which thoughts and anything else are arising. Nonthought must be defined inclusively, inseparable from the totality. It is important to transcend any effort to inhibit the arising of thought.

The thoughtless moment is a timeless moment, but Longchemba's instruction uses the phrase 'a necklace sequence of instants' that indicates each temporal perception as a window into its own transcendence, which, of course, is a provisional concept.

Compare this semdzin with 3/2, the semdzin of immediate emptiness. Can we usefully, rightfully, make a distinction between these states of nonthought and emptiness?

3/6 The Semdzin of Union

Zung jug la sems gzung ba ni: gnyis snang du shar dus gnyis 'dzin du 'char ba de rang la cher bltas pas rang dag gnyis med chen po'i nyams skye zhing yab yum gyi bde ba lam du byed pas kyang bde stong gnyis med kyi nyams skye'o.

The semdzin of union: At the arising of dualistic appearance, gaze intently at the crux of that polarity, and experience of the serene intrinsic purity of nonduality arises. By taking the bliss of male and female buddha-union as the path, the experience of nondual bliss and emptiness occurs.

NB: Union is 'co-incidence' (*zung 'jug*). This condition of two-in oneness is all our natural state. Meditate on alienation, on the sense of otherness, separateness. The moment of contact between sense and object: 'Catch the instant of union before the first instant of thought splits the moment into subject and object.'

Commentary
This semdzin is called the *zungjuk semdzin*, the semdzin of union. *Zungjuk* means 'arising together', 'arising as a pair', 'unity as inseparable duality', or 'co-incidence'. 'Union' is evidently not a precise translation of *zungjuk*, but to describe this semdzin as 'the semdzin of union' is adequate as a label, if not a descriptive phrase.

This semdzin has two aspects, the psychological and the psycho-sexual. Instruction on the first, the psychological aspect, is, 'Fixate at the point of dualistic grasping as dualistic appearances arise'. This refers to the union of subject and object, consciousness and the object of consciousness in sensory perception. In our ordinary dualistic functioning of perception, subject and object is the first manifestation of duality out of the unity that exists as the ground of all our minds. None of us are without it and experience of it happens constantly in the waking state. Thus we carry the ground of this semdzin around with us.

We are instructed to focus on the crux of duality which lies in the sensory organs where consciousness meets with the sensory object. Take the eye or the ear as the best basis, or we can take internal consciousness of thought or emotion as the focus. Look at the place where subject and object meet and there is unification; look at the place where dualities are unified. Do not look with your eyes, but be conscious of the screen upon which the object is projected. Do not judge, do not take a stand for or against anything, but be open to all. That is the nub of the instruction.

Particularly, the crux of subject and object, the unity, may be identified in the personal situation wherein we are alienated, or where we feel unintentionally attracted, one or the other, and where we can actually identify with the space where the division or attraction arises. The implication is that we can catch the unity in the moment of awareness of dualization, the moment in which otherness is objectified. Look at the moment of alienation, the moment of anger arising, the moment when separation in the process of aversion or attachment begins.

I think that any kind of psychological analysis here is useless.

Because while feeling ourselves as subject, we need an objective referent, implying a constant dualization, or objectification, in order to separate the one from the other. This is expressed more precisely as 'two-in-oneness', 'zungjuk', *yuganadha* in Sanskrit, which reveals the inadequacy of its expression as 'union'. Consider the use of the concept of 'oneness' in the Hindu context, where there is no differentiation within the experience, it is all happy and sameness and all distinctions are lost in the experience. In the tantric notion of two-in-oneness, the union, that sense of oneness in the union, the sameness, is the experiential ground, while subjectivity/objectivity, the characteristics of duality, are retained.

You may point out that in this semdzin the instruction demands what we call mirror-like awareness, 'awareness of the union of subject and object' which is a manner of stating buddha-enlightenment, and that there is no difference between unifying subject and object and the experience of *rikpa*. This is probably true. But how is it to be done? How do we follow such instruction, practically—technically—speaking? How do we stand in the union of clarity and awareness, of light and shade? The technique of this semdzin seems to be identification with the place of union of opposites. Nonaction, surely?

And, further, you may object, surely you are asking us to observe a metaphysical abstraction. We need to be convinced that this metaphysical abstraction can become an experiential reality where the dualities of light and darkness, of sun and moon, of good and bad, arise in a singular constellation, and that we can use it practically as a place of identity and perceive the lack of any distinction.

The second part of this semdzin is psycho-sexual. The-two-in-oneness can refer to the sexual union of man and woman (homosexual union requires a slightly different commentary). The instruction on the act of copulation is to identify with the 'ground' of union. We have 'the three recognitions' to assist in that process. The first is the recognition of sexual pleasure as the path; the second is the recognition of the self-liberation of pure pleasure as identification with the nature of mind; and thirdly recognition of the pure pleasure arising as emptiness.

Physical sexual union is the obvious application of this semdzin. 'When practising sexual yoga', instructs Longchemba, 'focus on the point of union'. If we understand 'the point of union' as the place of genital friction, then we are focusing upon the place where the tactile object meets consciousness. If sexual union is basically a sensory experience—and 'basic' here means 'as the ground'—then the tactile sense at the skin's most sensitive point is the place of concentration (or fixation). Sensory perceptivity is the basis of all our experience of sexual union. But, in metaphysical terminology, what we may call the essence of the experience is the union of male and female principles, which internally are emptiness and pure pleasure, or wisdom and compassion.

Why is this semdzin included here when its physicality seems to put it in another, totally different, category? Meditation on the five elements is the only other semdzin that requires application outside this room, off the meditation seat.

Certainly, several of the others can be practised outside, but our assumption is that the practice of these semdzins is a formal sitting practice. This yoga of union appears to be coming from a tantric source, relevant to tantric practitioners. The notion of two-in-oneness is present in Dzogchen precepts, as also is the metaphysics of the qualities that the right and left channels represent. But we must go to anuyoga and the mother-tantra in order to find the extraordinary significance of this practice in this context. It is within the mother-tantra that we find the answer to the question, Why are we emanated? Why are we embodied? Why male and female bodies with male and female sexually-specific physical paraphernalia? The answer may be that in our original non-dual condition, no duality, no polarity, gives us our gross sense of awareness. In the separate male and female embodiment of duality—polarity—we can unite and attain the awareness of two-in-oneness: what a nice piece of tantric sophistry!

But regardless of what we were talking about uniting opposites, then it is actually the physical duality of male and female in which the polarity is most poignantly and extremely expressed. If we are looking for the place of the transcendence of physical duality, then it is in sexual intimacy where the greatest potential arises and where it can best be discovered. Furthermore, this sexual instruction, this sexual metaphor in the text, sheds more light upon the abstract—nonphysical—potential of the meditation. It brings into focus the possibility of gender integration within the single psyche. Integration of male and female aspects of the mind—or male and female principles of the mind—is the natural state; and that is integrated guru and dakini within one mind.

3/7 The Semdzin of Space as the Path

Bar snang lam du byed ba ni: rig pa bar snang la yal yal song bar bsgom pa dang snang sems thams cad mkha'i dbyings na lding nge gang la'ang rten med du bsgom pa dang nam mkha' dang chos thams cad par bsgom pa ste. Mtha bral stong pa chen po'i nyams skye'o.

Taking space as the path: Visualize *rikpa* as identical to space and visualize all appearances and mind as floating in space unsupported, and visualize the sky as all things. Experience of the great emptiness without bounds arises.

CNN: Refer to Rushen HŪNG.

Commentary

This is the semdzin of taking space as the path. The space to be focused on in this semdzin is the space of the sky, the element that is space; this space is the space that is filled up by the other four elements. It is also like the empty space inside a vase. The instruction is again quite simple in form: 'Visualize everything, just as it is, floating in space'. This visualization includes our bodyminds and its sensory environment, and particularly the visual field. It includes all sounds, and all smells, and all tastes, and all tactile experience, and it includes all thought and emotion and all experience—mental, spiritual experience—whatsoever. It means the planet, the solar system and the universe. It entails conceptualizing *rikpa* as space.

If we have had this experience as a kind of initiatory experience, then to take it on as the path is quite easy. If we have not had that experience, then it is also quite easy to work with. Go back to the emptiness, the concentrated gaze into emptiness. This is not a fixed focused gaze at a point behind the object; rather it is a totally defocused gaze into the field that contains the object. Again, we are back to the ngondro exercise of the flying vajra, *that* space, because from a different angle we come to the experience of whatever arises, arises in that space. Through this practice, space becomes identical with the dharmadhatu, the space of emptiness, and we gain experience of the dharmadhatu. If we need conceptual references here, look at the blue HŪNGs. Look at the moment, first of all, the moment where the blue HŪNG is sitting in the torso, and then look at the moment when everything in the room or in the environment is filled with the blue HŪNG. And where are the blue HŪNGs sitting? And is the heart centre pure space? Or is it light? Or emptiness? Or awareness? Or thoughtlessness?

To all intent this space is the dharmadhatu, and this semdzin takes space as the path, takes the dharmadhatu as the path.

Appendix

Alternative Categorizations of the Semdzins

Semdzin for Experience of Emptiness

1/1	The Syllable PHAT: natural expression of mind as empty radiance [*sems stong gsal rang gdangs*]
2/2	Arrow and Noose: *rikpa* of empty radiance [*rig pa stong gsal*]
2/5	Transference: thought-free emptiness [*stong nyid bsam mno dang bral ba*]
3/1	Gradual Emptiness: nondual emptiness and appearances [*snang stong pa gnyis su med pa*]
3/2	Immediate Emptiness: all appearances like condensation on a mirror [*snang ba thams cad me long la has btab pa lta bu*]
3/6	Union: empty bliss [*bde stong*]
3/7	Space: ultimate super-emptiness [*mtha' bral stong pa chen po*]

Semdzin for Experience of Thoughtlessness

1/1	White 'A' beyond thought and no thought: [*sems spro bsdu dang bral ba*]
1/3	Heruka's Laughter: thoughtless radiance [*rtog med gsal gdams*]
1/4	Titan's Struggle: self-liberating vision [*mthong snang rang grol*]
1/7	Thought-Pursuing HŪNGs: [*rnam rtog chos nyid du sangs pa*]
2/3	White Sphere: thoughtless radiance [*rtog med gsal ba*]
3/3	Impermanence: free of reference [*gza' gtad dang bral ba*]
3/5	Nonthought: thoughtless hyper-being [*rtog med rang gnas chen po*]

Semdzin for Experience of Clarity

1/2	Syllable PHAT: [*sems stong gsal rang gdangs*]
1/3	Heruka's Laughter: [*rtog med gsal gdams*]
1/5	Thought-pursuing HŪNGs: [*rnam rtog chos nyid du sangs pa*)
1/7	Vajrasattva: [*shes pa gsal dag chen po*]

2/2	Three Staffs: [*rig pa stong gsal*]
2/3	White Sphere: [*rtog med gsal ba*]
2/4	Rainbow Body: [*'od gsal dag pa*]
2/7	Heart Samantabhadra: [*'od gsal dag pa*]

Semdzin for Experience of Self-liberating Phenomena

1/4	Titan's Struggle: [*mthong snang rang grol*]
1/7	Kunzang in the Heart
3/4	Five Elements

Semdzin for Experience of Freedom from Grasping

3/3	Impermanence: freedom from reference points [*gza' gtad dang bral ba*]

Other Categories of Semdzin:

Employing glottal 'A': 1/1, 2/4
Exclamations: PHAT 1/2, HŪNG 1/5, 2/5, HA 1/3
Visualizing *lha sku*: 1/7, (2/6), 2/7,
Visualizing *thig le*: 2/1, 1/3, 1/4, 1/5, 1/7
Focusing on breath: 1/1, 1/5, 1/7, 2/2,
Formless meditation: 3/2, 3/3, 3/4, 3/5, 3/6, 3/7
Thought-cutting: 1/2, 1/3, 1/5, (3/5)

Other Titles from Keith Dowman

Padma Publishing
Nepal Mandal: The Powerplaces of the Kathmandu Valley (forthcoming)

Dzogchen Now! Books
Dzogchen: A Matter of Mind.
Everything is Light: A *Great Explanatory Dzogchen Tantra, The Circle of Total Illumination.*
The Circle of Total Illumination: The Epitome
Guru Pema Here and Now: The Mythology of the Lotus-Born.
The Yeshe Lama: Jigmelingpa's Dzogchen Manual.
Spaciousness: The Radical Dzogchen of the Vajra-Heart (Longchemba).
Maya Yoga: Finding Comfort and Ease in Enchantment (Longchemba).
The Nyingma Icons
The Divine Madman: The Life and Songs of Drukpa Kunley.

Commercial Publications
Original Perfection: Vairotsana's Five Early Transmissions, Wisdom.   Also,
The Eye of the Storm, Vajra Books.
The Great Secret of Mind: Instruction on Nonduality in Dzogchen
      (Tulku Pema Riktsal), Shambhala.
Natural Perfection (Longchemba), Wisdom Publications.
      Also, *Old Man Basking in the Sun*, Vajra Books.
The Flight of the Garuda (Shabkar Rinpoche) Wisdom.
The Sacred Life of Tibet, HarperCollins.
Power-Places of Kathmandu, Inner Traditions.
Boudhanath: The Great Stupa.
Masters of Enchantment, Inner Traditions.
The Power-Places of Central Tibet: The Pilgrims Guide, RKP,
      Pilgrims, Vajra Books.
Masters of Mahamudra, SUNY.
Sky Dancer: The Secret Life and Songs of the Lady Yeshe Tsogyal,
      Penguin, Shambhala.
The Legend of the Great Stupa, Dharma Publishing.
Calm and Clear: A Manual of Buddhist Meditation, Dharma Publishing.

See www.keithdowman.net and www.radicaldzogchen.com for details of
publications and the public talks of
Keith Dowman.

FINI

Made in the USA
Columbia, SC
27 February 2020

88476782R00050